BAPTISM

WITH THE

HOLY GHOST

by

Henry Clay Morrison

First Fruits Press
Wilmore, Kentucky
c2012

asburyseminary.edu
800.2ASBURY
204 North Lexington Avenue
Wilmore, Kentucky 40390

First Fruits
THE ACADEMIC OPEN PRESS OF ASBURY SEMINARY

ISBN: 9780984738786

Baptism with the Holy Ghost, by Henry Clay Morrison.
First Fruits Press, © 2012
Pentecostal Publishing Company, © 1900

Digital version at http://place.asburyseminary.edu/firstfruitsheritagematerial/1/

For all other uses, contact:

First Fruits Press
B.L. Fisher Library
Asbury Theological Seminary
204 N. Lexington Ave.
Wilmore, KY 40390
http://place.asburyseminary.edu/firstfruits

Morrison, H. C. (Henry Clay), 1857-1942.
    Baptism with the Holy Ghost / by Henry Clay Morrison.
    Wilmore, Ky. : First Fruits Press, c2012.
    39 p. ; 21 cm.
    Reprint. Previously published: Louisville, Ky. : Pentecostal Publishing
    Company, c1900.
    ISBN: 9780984738786 (pbk.)
    1. Baptism in the Holy Spirit. 2. Holy Spirit. 3. Sanctification. I. Title.
BT123 .M57 2012

Cover design by Haley Hill

asburyseminary.edu
800.2ASBURY
204 North Lexington Avenue
Wilmore, Kentucky 40390

First Fruits
THE ACADEMIC OPEN PRESS OF ASBURY SEMINARY

BAPTISM

WITH THE

HOLY GHOST

BY

Rev. H. C. MORRISON

—

PENTECOSTAL PUBLISHING COMPANY
Louisville, Kentucky

PREFACE

It is scarcely worth while to say to the reader that in this booklet on "The Baptism with the Holy Ghost," I have not attempted anything exhaustive, but have tried to set forth an important Bible truth in a plain, simple way. I have often wished for a booklet on this subject so cheap that the poor could buy it, so small that the busy could read it, and so plain that those of the most ordinary learning and intelligence could understand it. I have preached the truth herein contained to many thousands of people, and God has graciously put the seal of His approval on the Word in the conversion of a multitude of sinners, and the sanctification of many believers. I send it out with the prayer that God may make it a blessing to many, and with the request that those who read it with profit will pass it on to others.

Your brother,

H. C. MORRISON.

STATING THE CASE

In discussing the important doctrine of the Baptism with the Holy Ghost, I wish first of all, to state the case; then I shall introduce the inspired witnesses and argue the case from the testimony given by them.

(1) In the great scheme of human redemption God has provided that all of His children may receive the baptism with the Holy Ghost.

(2) The baptism with the Holy Ghost is bestowed subsequent to regeneration; not at, but after pardon.

(3) The baptism with the Holy Ghost is for believers only, and is never bestowed upon the unregenerate.

(4) The baptism with the Holy Ghost purifies believers' hearts, and empowers them for service.

(5) The Holy Ghost dwells in, abides with, comforts and teaches those who receive Him.

(6) The rejection of the Holy Ghost is fatal to Christian experience.

It will be appropriate just here to call attention to the fact that the Holy Ghost is a person.

He is the third person in the Trinity, and is one with the Father and the Son, equal with them in eternity, holiness and honor.

This fact is plainly taught in the Scriptures, especially in administering the rite of baptism, and in the apostolic benediction. See Matt. 28:19: "Go ye therefore and teach all nations, baptizing them in the name of the Father, and of the Son, and of the Holy Ghost."

In the closing verse of the last chapter of his second epistle to the Corinthians, St. Paul fully recognizes the equality of the Holy Ghost with the Father, and the Son, in these impressive, beautiful words of benediction: "The grace of the Lord Jesus Christ, and the love of God, and the communion of the Holy Ghost, be with you all. Amen."

All of Christ's sayings about the Holy Ghost, prove His personality. Take for example, John 16:7. "It is expedient for you that I go away: for if I go not away, the Comforter will not come unto you; but if I depart, I will send *Him* unto you." Notice here the pronoun—Him.

It is never proper or scriptural to speak of the Holy Ghost as a thing, but always as a person. Then let us bear in mind that the Holy Ghost is as essentially a person as is Jesus Christ, and that as certainly as Jesus made His advent into the world in Bethlehem, the Holy Ghost made His advent into the world at Jerusalem, on the day of Pentecost, and that the times in which we live are especially the dispensation of the Holy Ghost.

We will now consider the first proposition in the statement of the case. *"In the great scheme of human redemption, God has provided that all of His children may receive the baptism with the Holy Ghost."*

When John the Baptist came preaching in the wilderness, the burden of his message was the coming Christ, and the baptism he would bestow. Only those who believed John's message, received

John's baptism, and all of them were assured that when Christ came they should receive from Him another baptism.

"I indeed baptize you with water unto repentance: but He that cometh after me is mightier than I, whose shoes I am not worthy to bear: He shall baptize you with the Holy Ghost and with fire." Matt. 3:11. John administered water baptism with the distinct understanding that the baptism he gave was but a preparation for the greater baptism of the Holy Ghost, which Christ would administer when He came. I have never been able to understand how it is that persons can receive John's testimony with regard to water baptism, and reject it with regard to the baptism with the Holy Ghost, for as certainly as John administered the one, he promised that Christ should administer the other.

So far as John's testimony is concerned, the baptism with the Holy Ghost is Christ's prime credential, proving His Messiahship. After John's definite declaration that Christ would bestow the baptism with the Holy Ghost, if Christ had not bestowed him, John's testimony would have fallen to the ground. Let us suppose that an intelligent, though sinful Jew, attends upon the ministry of the great wilderness preacher. As John speaks his awful denunciation against sin, crying, "Oh, generation of vipers," and declaring that the "ax is laid unto the root of the trees," and that every tree which bringeth not forth good fruit shall be hewn down and cast into the fire, this Jew is made to tremble because of his sins. He believes the message, the Messiah is coming. He forsakes his sins, and with faith in the Christ that John is preaching, he asks baptism at the hands of John. John baptizes him and says to him, "He that cometh after me is mightier than I, whose shoes I am not worthy to bear: He shall baptize you with the Holy Ghost, and with fire."

Could this Jew ever forget the promise of John? Would he not say to his friends, "John has baptized me with water, but he has promised me another and greater baptism, which I shall receive from Christ who is greater than John!" Would not that Jew naturally believe that in proportion as Christ is greater than John, the baptism with the Holy Ghost, which Christ administers, is superior to the baptism of water, which John administers? When Jesus appears, will not this Jew, if he be a true believer in John, follow Jesus, expecting to receive from Him the baptism with the Holy Ghost? Most assuredly he will. That is exactly what they did do. John fully understood the situation. John willingly gave up his disciples that they might follow Jesus. He said: "He must increase, but I must decrease."

These disciples of John had been instructed by him that he was only a herald of the coming King, that Jesus was the true Messiah, and He it was that should baptize them with the Holy Ghost and with fire; and they followed Jesus with no other expectation than that they should receive from Him this baptism; and they were not disappointed.

After the promise made by John, if Jesus had

said nothing of the baptism with the Holy Ghost, those who followed Him, full of faith and expectation, would have been forced to the conclusion that John was a false prophet, and that Christ was not the true Messiah; but they were not doomed to disappointment.

John was a true prophet, and Christ was the Son of God, and what John promised, Christ graciously bestowed.

The disciples had not followed Jesus long until He confirmed John's testimony concerning Himself. It was on the last day, that great day of the feast, Jesus stood and cried, saying, "If any man thirst let him come unto me, and drink. He that believeth on me, as the Scripture hath said, out of his belly shall flow rivers of living water. But this spake He of the Spirit, which they that believe on Him should receive: for the Holy Ghost was not yet given; because that Jesus was not yet glorified."

From these Scriptures we learn that the Holy Ghost was to be given to those who *believe* on Christ. This **gift** of the Spirit was not limited to the apostles. Notice the breadth of the promise: *"If any man thirst,   He that believeth on me,   They that believe on Him should receive."* This promise takes in all believers. It is a narrow and unscriptural view that limits the baptism with the Holy Ghost to the apostles only. These plain words of Jesus, *"Any man," "Him that believeth," "They that believe,"* sweep away all barriers that men would erect between God's children and the baptism with the Holy Ghost, and teach unmistakably that this divine baptism is for all of God's children. We notice that Christ repeats the promise of the gift of the Holy Ghost in John 14:16.

Jesus had just said to His disciples, "Whither I go ye cannot come." This filled their hearts with sorrow, and He comforted them with those immortal and sure words of promise, found in John 14. "Let not your heart be troubled; ye believe in God, believe also in me. In my Father's house are many mansions: if it were not so, I would have told you. I go to prepare a place for you. And if I go and prepare a place for you, I will come again, and receive you unto myself; that where I am, there ye may be also."

But God had provided still more fully for their comfort, and Jesus said to them: "If ye love me, keep my commandments. And I will pray the Father, and He shall give you another Comforter, that he may abide with you forever; Even the Spirit of truth; whom the world cannot receive, because it seeth Him not, neither knoweth Him: but ye know Him; for He dwelleth with you, and shall be in you."

In the twenty-sixth verse of the same chapter, Jesus tells the disciples that this Comforter, whom the Father will send, is the Holy Ghost. It was after the resurrection, and just before His ascension, that Jesus further confirmed the prophecy of John, and the promises which He had previously made his disciples. See Acts 1:4, 5. "And being assembled together with them, commanded them that they should not depart from

Jerusalem, but wait for the promise of the Father, which, saith He, ye have heard of me: For John truly baptized with water; but ye shall be baptized with the Holy Ghost, not many days hence."

These words are plain and easy of comprehension. *Command* and *promise* could not be more specific.

The pledge of the gift of the Holy Ghost, of which the disciples have heard so much, in which they are bound to be so deeply interested, is vouchsafed in unmistakable language.

In obedience to the *commandment*, and with faith in the *promise*, the disciples tarried at Jerusalem. The protracted waiting in the upper room while ten days passed by, shows an obedience and faith in the early disciples which modern, impatient professors of discipleship will do well to imitate.

No doubt in these long days of waiting by the faithful hundred and twenty, there is a valuable lesson for us. There must be in the disciple of Christ a spirit of genuine submission, obedience, and faith, that will tarry in patient waiting so long as the Lord may see fit to tarry in His coming.

When Christ gives a commandment to wait and promises a blessing for those who do wait, we must learn to wait, and to wait without murmur or complaint, until the promised blessing comes. The disciples waited, and not in vain; for, "when the day of Pentecost was fully come, they were all with *one accord* in one place." How fortunate they were "with one accord." No rebellious spir-

it, or unbelieving heart, broke the harmony of
that glad, humble, patient group, who waited in
the upper room.

There is a peculiar blessing in the *mutual*
faith of those who love the Lord. In Rom. 1:11,
12, Paul says, "For I long to see you, that I may
impart unto you some spiritual gift. to the end ye
may be established. That is, that I may be comforted together with you by the mutual faith both
of you and me."

Those who do not believe in, or seek for the
Holy Ghost, but rather oppose those who do, will
not know the damage they have done the church,
or the hurt they have been to the cause of Christ,
until the books are opened at the last day.

The inspired record says, "And *suddenly*
(reader, mark that word '*suddenly*.' It is thus
that the Spirit comes upon believers) there came
a sound from heaven, as of a rushing mighty
wind, and it filled all the house where they were
sitting. And there appeared unto them cloven
tongues, like as of fire, and it sat upon each of
them. And they were all filled with the Holy
Ghost." John's prophecy was fulfilled, and
Christ's promise was kept, in this wonderful baptism with the Holy Ghost. Without doubt John
was a true prophet, and Jesus of Nazareth is the
true Messiah, the world's Redeemer. The disci
ples are confirmed, the world is convinced, sinners
are convicted, and three thousand souls are converted on the spot.

Lest some one should say this baptism with
the Holy Ghost was only a temporary gift to the

church, or a special gift to the early Christians, God, in His wisdom, put into Peter's mouth words that are plain and unmistakable. "Then Peter said unto them, Repent, and be baptized, every one of you in the name of Jesus Christ for the remission of sins, and ye shall receive the gift of the Holy Ghost." Acts 2:38.

These words of Peter were addressed to the three thousand who, being pricked in their hearts, had said, "Men and brethren, what shall we do?"

St. Peter encourages them with the following words of assurance: "For the promise is unto you. and to your children, and to all that are afar off, even as many as the Lord our God shall call."

Could a promise be stated more plainly, or be more comprehensive?

The baptism with the Holy Ghost was for the eleven apostles, for the one hundred and nine persons in the upper room with them, for the three thousand to be bestowed after they had received remission of sins, for the children of the three thousand, for ALL that are afar off, even as MANY as the Lord our God shall call. The word "call" here evidently means convert, or pardon, or regenerate. Even as many as God shall regenerate, have the promise of the baptism with the Holy Ghost.

Beloved reader, with these plain Scriptures before us there is but one reasonable conclusion at which we can arrive, and that is, *that in the great scheme of human redemption, God has provided that all of His children may receive the baptism with the Holy Ghost.*

Permit me to close this chapter, by addressing to you the words of the Apostle Paul to the young converts at Ephesus:

"Have ye received the Holy Ghost SINCE ye believed?" If not, it is not because there is not abundant provision made in the atonement, and oft-repeated promises of such a baptism contained in the Scriptures.

WHEN OBTAINED

The baptism with the Holy Ghost is bestowed subsequent to regeneration; not at, but after pardon.

The above statement is not only abundantly taught in the Scriptures, but is strikingly illustrated in the case of the apostles, and those believers who were with them in the upper room at the time of their receiving the baptism with the Spirit.

I am aware that some persons, when hard pressed in their efforts to prove that the baptism with the Holy Ghost received on the day of Pentecost was not a blessing received subsequent to regeneration, have contended that the apostles and their companions were only converted on that occasion. The fallacy of such reasoning is quite plain when we refer to the following Scriptures.

I call attention first, to Luke 10:20, where Jesus said to the disciples, "Rejoice not, that the spirits are subject unto you; but rather rejoice, because your names are written in heaven." Now we know that evil spirits are not subject to sinners, but sinners are subject to the evil spirits; but the evil spirits were subject to the disciples; therefore the disciples were not sinners. We know also that sinners' names are not written in heaven, but the disciples' names were written in heaven. Therefore the disciples were not sinners. Now, when we remember that the words of Jesus quoted above was uttered some months before the baptism at Pentecost, we are forced to the conclusion that the disciples were pardoned, regenerated men, long before they received the baptism with the Holy Ghost.

We also read in John 17:12, "While I was with them in the world, I kept them in thy name; those that thou gavest me I have kept, and none of them is lost, but the son of perdition." If none of them were lost but Judas, then the eleven disciples were saved; but unpardoned sinners are lost, therefore the disciples were not sinners. Judas himself had once been in a pardoned state, for the Scriptures say that "Judas by transgression fell." Had this unfortunate man not been in a state of grace, he could not have fallen. In the sixteenth verse of the same chapter, Jesus says, "They are not of the world, even as I am not of the world."

When we remember that all these sayings of our Lord took place some time before Pentecost, we cannot believe any candid mind will ask for further proof that the disciples were regenerated men long before their sanctification by the baptism with the Holy Ghost.

We call attention to the history of the revival at Samaria, held by the Evangelist Philip. This was a genuine work of grace. "The people with one accord gave heed to the things which Philip spake." "Unclean spirits, crying with a loud voice came out of many that were possessed with them." "And there was great joy in the city." The reader may be sure that the *great joy* was not among the sinners, who rejected

Philip's message. Those who rejoiced were doubtless of the number out of whom the unclean spirits had been cast, and others who, believing the Gospel message, had forsaken their sins and accepted Christ.

No Bible Christian will question the excellence and thoroughness of the work done in this revival.

"But when they believed Philip preaching the things concerning the kingdom of God, and the name of Jesus Christ, they were baptized, both men and women." Acts 8:12.

No language will express what followed so well as Luke's own inspired words. Hence we quote him: "Now, when the apostles which were at Jerusalem heard that Samaria had received the word of God, they sent unto them Peter and John: who, when they were come down, *prayed for them, that they might receive the Holy Ghost. For as yet He was fallen upon none of them.*" There it is, honest reader. They had received the word, believed in Jesus, the unclean spirits had been cast out of them, they had great joy, and had been baptized. *Who will dare say they were not pardoned?* But they had not yet received the Holy Ghost. But when Peter and John prayed for them that they might receive the Holy Ghost, and laid their hands on them, they did receive the Holy Ghost. *All must agree that this baptism with the Holy Ghost was subsequent to regeneration.* Nothing could be plainer.

Now, let us take the case of Cornelius. That this man was a pardoned man prior to Peter's visit to him, and the falling of the Holy Ghost upon him, we cannot understand how anyone can doubt. The Scripture says of Cornelius that he was *"A devout man,"*   *"one that feared God, with all his house,"*   *" gave much alms,"* *"and prayed to God alway."* The angel who visited him said, "Thy prayers and thine alms are come up for a memorial before God."

Can anyone doubt this man's Christianity? Can the reader conceive of a *"devout"* sinner, "fearing God, *with all his house?"* This man's piety had drawn his family with him into the love and service of God.

"The sacrifice of the wicked is an abomination to the Lord, but the prayer of the upright is his delight." Prov. 15:8.

Had Cornelius been a wicked man his prayer and alms would not have come up for a memorial before the Lord. But his alms were accepted, therefore he was not a sinner.

"He that turneth away his ear from the hearing of the law, even his prayer shall be abomination." Prov. 28:9.

But the prayers of Cornelius were pleasing to God, therefore he did not turn away his ear from hearing of the law, but was obedient, devout, upright.

Take the testimony of Peter himself, on his meeting and salutation of Cornelius. "Of a truth I perceive that God is no respecter of persons. But in every nation he that *feareth* Him, and *worketh righteousness is accepted with Him."*

What need have we of further proof, that this man is a servant of God, of a very high order?

Sinners do not *"fear"* God, *"and work right-eousness,"* neither are sinners *"accepted with him."* But Cornelius was accepted with the God he feared, obeyed and worshipped, therefore he was not a sinner, but a Christian. His sins had been pardoned, he was justified before God, *"accepted with Him."* But he had not yet received the baptism with the Holy Ghost, for this baptism is a blessing bestowed, not before, or at the time of justification, but subsequent to it.

While Peter preached to this *"devout,"* *prayer-ful, charitable, righteous, obedient, God-fearing man*, the Holy Ghost fell on him and his God-fearing household, purifying their hearts. We could not wish for a clearer case of sanctification, by the baptism with the Holy Ghost, subsequent to regeneration.

I could give other instances, and quote other Scriptures, but if these Scriptures given do not convince the reader beyond all doubt and cavil that the baptism with the Holy Ghost is bestowed subsequent to regeneration, not at, but after pardon, it seems to me that with such an one an appeal to Scripture is useless.

To every humble, believing heart, I will say, The Comforter is promised you. Tarry at the mercy seat in faithful prayer until you receive the gift of the Holy Ghost. Through all the history of the Church of Christ, witnesses can be found who will gladly testify from personal experience, that the promise was not restricted to the few, but was vouchsafed to "all" that were "afar off, even as many as the Lord our God shall call." "Seek and ye shall find, ask and ye shall receive."

WHO IT IS FOR

The baptism with the Holy Ghost is for believers only, and is never bestowed upon the unregenerated.

Shortly before Jesus was crucified he promised His disciples that the indwelling, abiding Holy Ghost should be their Comforter. "Even the spirit of truth," said He, "Whom the world cannot receive, because it seeth him not, neither knoweth him." The term "world," here refers to the unregenerated, and Jesus says of them that they cannot receive the Holy Ghost.

This fully explains the opposition to the Holy Ghost, and his manifestations among many professed Christians. They either have never been converted, or they have fallen away into a sinful, cold, formal life ,and have ceased to be the true children of the Father. When Jesus came in the flesh to the Jewish church, only those who were Israelites indeed recognized and received Him as the Son of God. The chief priests and scribes could not understand that Jesus was the Messiah even when He healed the sick and raised the dead.

Simeon and Anna, the prophetess, had no trouble recognizing Him, even when He was a helpless babe in His mother's arms. "The secret of the Lord is with them that fear Him." Jesus Himself said of the unbelieving Jews: "He that is of God heareth God's word: ye therefore hear them not, because ye are not of God." John

8:47. Again, in 1 John 4:6, Jesus says: "He that knoweth God heareth us; he that is not of God heareth not us. Hereby know we the spirit of truth and the spirit of error."

Just as the unbelieving and godless Jews in the church under the old dispensation rejected Jesus, so do the unconverted and backslidden in the Christian church under the new dispensation reject the Holy Ghost.

There is not only the provision in the Gospel for the gift of the Holy Ghost to purify and comfort believing hearts, but there is in truly regenerated hearts a crying out for the gift of the Holy Ghost, an inward longing for the Comforter. Jesus calls it "hungering and thirsting after righteousness." It was to this class that He addressed himself on the last great day of the feast, when He said, "If any man thirst let Him come unto me and drink. .   This spake he of the Spirit, which they that believe on Him should receive. For the Holy Ghost was not yet given."

Sinners in the church know full well that the Holy Ghost has His place in the Scriptures. They are willing for him to have a place in creeds and confessions. He may even be alluded to in songs and sermons, but they would shut Him out of the hearts of men. They object to His demonstrations and manifestations. This is so, because spiritual things are spiritually discerned, and they have no spiritual discernment. The unregenerated cannot receive the spirit of truth, "because" they "see him not, neither know him." And now, O reader, if you have not received the Holy Ghost, and have no longing desire for Him, at least at certain periods in your life, without doubt you are in an unpardoned state.   And I must close this chapter by addressing you in the language of the Apostle Paul to Simon the Sorcerer: "I perceive that thou art in the gall of bitterness, and in the bond of iniquity."   May the mercy of God bring thee to a speedy and sincere repentance.

WHO ARE ELIGIBLE

The baptism with the Holy Ghost purifies believers' hearts and empowers them for service.

Uncleanness remains in the hearts of pardoned believers. This is clearly taught in the Scriptures and sadly experienced by Christians; not only by the early followers of Jesus, but all who come into the kingdom of God by faith, find remaining within themselves a root of bitterness, a strong tendency to evil, a proneness to wander from the God they love.

Paul calls this remaining uncleanness, "Sin that dwelleth in me," "The carnal mind," "Our old man" and, "The body of death."

This "filthiness of flesh and spirit" remaining in believers greatly impedes their Christian growth, and hinders their usefulness. It manifests itself in unholy pride, vicious tempers, covetous desires, unclean thoughts and imaginations. The soul struggling with this inward enemy is often made to cry out: "Oh wretched man that I am, who shall deliver me from the body of this death?"

Only those who are truly justified, and are striving to live a New Testament life in *look* and *thought,* are acquainted with these internal conflicts with the "Old man."

The unregenerated and the backslidden in the churches are so under the dominion of this evil nature, the "Old man," that they have no conflict with him but are under the sway of his dominion, humor his whims, gratify his lusts and feed his appetites. It is those who have passed from death to life, and are striving after holiness in heart and practice, who find within themselves "a law that, when" they "would do good, evil is present with" them. They learn to their sorrow that the carnal mind is within them, and that "the carnal mind is enmity against God." Writing to the Corinthians in the first verses of the third chapter, Paul declares the situation very plainly: "And I, brethren, could not speak unto you as unto spiritual, but as unto *carnal*, even as unto *babes in Christ*. I have fed you with milk, and not with meat; for hitherto ye were not able to bear it, neither yet now are ye able. *For ye are yet carnal!*"

The reader will notice that these Corinthians were *"brethren."* Yes, they were *"Babes in Christ."* But they *yet* had the carnal mind in them. *"For ye are yet carnal,"* says the apostle.

What clearer testimony could the Holy Ghost give than this to the fact, that the carnal mind remains in those who have been born again? These *brethren* could not have been babes in Christ if they had not have been born again. But they were babes in Christ so without doubt they had been born again, born of the Spirit, *yet* they were carnal, *the carnal mind remained in them.*

How true to experience are the inspired statements found in Romans 7:21, 22, 23: "I find then a law, that when I would do good, evil is present with me. For I delight in the law of God after the inward man. But I see another law in my members warring against the law of my mind."

Observe here that the inward man *delights in the law of God.* The sinner has no inward man except the "old man," and you may be sure the "old man" does not delight in the law of God. The inward man spoken of here is the regenerated man, the new man, imparted by the grace of God to the penitent sinner by regenerating grace, at the time of his justification. This *new "inward man,"* delights in the law of God, but the "old man" remaining in the nature makes war on the new man, and when the *new man* would do good, the "old man," (evil) is present with him, to hinder him in carrying out his good intentions.

The Christian reader will at once recognize the undoubted truthfulness of these Scriptures for they are corroborated by the every-day experience of believing souls, who, struggling against the "old man," have often been made to cry out. "O wretched man that I am, who shall deliver me from the body of this death." The baptism with the Holy Ghost casts out the "old man." And the casting out of the "old man," the plucking up of the root of bitterness, the destruction of the body of sin, the eradication of the carnal mind, the purging out of "the sin that dwelleth in me," are all one and the same thing, which is accomplished by the instantaneous baptism with the Holy Ghost, purifying the heart by faith. *This is entire sanctification.*

This purifying of hearts took place with the disciples on the day of Pentecost, when they received the baptism with the Holy Ghost. Not only do their after lives, as contrasted with their former behavior, manifest this to be true, but Peter bears testimony to this fact in relating his experience with Cornelius and his household. "And God, which knoweth the hearts, bear them witness, giving them the Holy Ghost, even as He did unto us; And put no difference between us and them, *purifying their hearts by faith."* Acts 15:8, 9. Peter is here referring to the baptism with the Holy Ghost, which fell upon the household of Cornelius and the exact similarity between it and the baptism received by the disciples on the day of Pentecost. The one important feature of the baptism to which he calls attention was the PURIFYING of their HEARTS.

When Jesus was present with the disciples assembled in Jerusalem after His resurrection, and commanded them not to depart out of Jerusalem until they received the promise of the Father, He said unto them: "But ye shall receive power after that the Holy Ghost is come upon you."

This enduement of power was to especially qualify them, not only for their life work, but for personal victory over Satan and sin. This enduement of power which is to be obtained only by the baptism with the Holy Ghost, is the great need of the church in the times in which we live, not only for those who stand in the sacred desk, but for those who sit in the pews also. The work of winning souls from sin to Christ is not shut up alone to ministers of the Gospel, but it is the duty and privilege of all saved souls to win lost souls to the Savior. It seems like a dangerous and arrogant presumption to undertake the work of Christ and, at the same time, refuse to apply to Him for that *Power* which He has definitely promised, and which we so manifestly need. It is a sad sight to see an institution claiming to be a church of God undertake to do with organizations, entertainments and festivals the work that can only be done by the enduement of power which comes with the baptism with the Holy Ghost. No natural gifts, mental developments or scholastic training can possibly take the place of the divine energy and unction which alone can be imparted to men by the gift of the Holy Ghost. "We wrestle not," says the apostle Paul, "against flesh and blood, but against principalities, against powers, against the rulers of the darkness of this world, against spiritual wickedness in high places."

Reader, shall we go forth to do battle against these mighty foes in our strength, or shall we tarry in humble, faithful prayer for the coming of the Holy Ghost, and the *Power* which His coming brings? If we wait in humble prayer until we receive Him, then doubtless it can be said of us, "Greater is He that is in you, than he that is in the world." If we must go forth to war against devils and mighty evil spirits! If we must meet in combat the prince of the power of the air, let us meet them endued with the power of the indwelling Holy Ghost.

When men enlist as soldiers in the services of the kingdoms of this world, the government for which they fight is expected to furnish them with arms and ammunition. Those who enlist in the services of the King of kings may be sure that He will not ask them to go to war without equipment, and that equipment will be an "enduement of *power* from on high," received in the baptism with the Holy Ghost.

WHAT HE DOES

The Holy Ghost dwells in, abides with, comforts and teaches those who receive Him.

(1) The baptism with the Holy Ghost inaugurates between the redeemed soul and the eternal Father the most intimate and sacred relations. The human body out of which the carnal mind has been cast, at once becomes the temple of the Holy Spirit. "Know ye not that ye are the temple of God, and that the Spirit of God dwelleth in you?" 1 Cor. 3:16. Again, in the same epistle, 6:19, we read: "What know ye not that your body is the temple of the Holy Ghost which is in you, which ye have of God, and ye are not your own?"

The kingdom of God is "within you." Luke 17:21. "The kingdom of God is not meat and drink, but righteousness, and peace, and joy in the Holy Ghost." Rom. 14:17. When our Lord promised the disciples that He would pray the Father to send them another Comforter, *"even the Spirit of truth,"* He assured them that the world could not receive this Spirit, "Because it seeth Him not, neither knoweth Him; but ye know Him; for He dwelleth with you, and *Shall Be In You.*" One of the best preventives against temptation and sin for those who have received the baptism with the Holy Ghost, is the constant memory that God, in the person of the Holy Ghost, is *dwelling in them.* The thought will keep out all desire for sin, and break the power of the tempter. It will constantly gird up the soul with a blessed assurance of victory, knowing that He that is in us is greater than he that is in the world.

(2)   I call the reader's attention to the fact that when the Holy Ghost comes into His temples, our bodies, and purifies them, He comes "to abide forever."

When Jesus said to His disciples, "Ye shall seek me; and as I said unto the Jews, Whither I go ye cannot come, so now I say to you," their hearts were filled with sadness, and He comforted them with the promise that He would prepare a place for them, and come again and receive them unto Himself, that where He was, there they might be also.

He further assured them that if they loved Him and would keep His commandments, He would pray the Father, and He would give them another Comforter, *"That He may abide with you forever."*

Christ made it a point to put in this word "forever" for the good reason that He desired the disciples to be encouraged with the assurance that the Holy Ghost would abide, not only in the Church, but in the individual who received Him, not for a few brief years, as He had done, and then grieve their hearts by separating himself from them as He, their Lord, must now soon do, but the Comforter would *abide*.   There would be no more painful separation like that for which He was now preparing them, which must take place in a few days.

(3)   The Holy Ghost should not only be a purifier ((being sanctified by the Holy Ghost), an *indweller, abiding forever*, but He should also be

a *Comforter*. This is an important office of the Spirit, the comforting of the hearts of God's children. In sickness, in poverty, in trials and persecutions, when deserted by friends and pursued by enemies, when in a strange land, and in all the conflicts and vicissitudes of life, the blessed Spirit abiding in the heart constantly gives assurance of His presence, of the salvation of the soul, of the love of God for it, of the efficacy of the cleansing blood of Jesus Christ, and thus keeps the soul in a state of blessed comfort.

Let those who have cried to God for comfort in times of distress, learn to cry to God for the gift of the Holy Ghost, and then they will have the abiding Comforter within themselves.

(4) Christ not only promised that the abiding Spirit should comfort, but that He should also be our *teacher*. In John 14:26 He says: "But the Comforter, which is the Holy Ghost, whom the Father will send in my name, He shall teach you all things and bring all things to your remembrance, whatsoever I have said unto you."

Again, John 16:13, 14, our Lord says: "Howbeit when He, the Spirit of truth, is come, He will guide you into all truth; for He shall not speak of Himself, but whatsoever He shall hear, that shall He speak, and He will show you things to come. He shall glorify me; for He shall receive of mine, and shall show it unto you."

With these Scriptures before us, the reader will appreciate something of the importance of the baptism with the Holy Ghost, and the various offices He performs in the redemption of the souls of men.

HIS INDWELLING

The rejection of the Holy Ghost is fatal to Christian experiences.

The greatest sin in past history was the rejection of Jesus Christ by the church under the old dispensation. Often our minds have been amazed and our hearts have shuddered as we have read: "He came unto His own and His own received Him not." We have marveled at the stupidity and hardness of the Jews, who looked in the face of Jesus of Nazareth, heard His words, beheld His miracles, and yet ridiculed and rejected Him.

Reader, think you that those ancient Jews were sinners above all men? I tell you they were not, and without doubt those members of the Christian Church under the new dispensation who reject the Holy Ghost, will commit even more grievous and fatal sin than that committed by the Jews in rejecting Christ. In proportion as our light is greater than was theirs, our sin will be more inexcusable than theirs. In the final day of judgment I would as soon stand there an ancient Jew who rejected Jesus, as to stand there a modern Gentile who rejected the Holy Ghost. In fact, to reject the Holy Ghost is to reject the Father and the Son, also. To come to the actual truth, those Jews who really had the Father, did not reject the Son, but, like Simeon and Nathaniel, they recognized and worshipped Him.

So it is with those who really have the forgiveness of their sins and true fellowship with Jesus

Christ. They will, if properly instructed, gladly receive the Holy Ghost for whom the Son prayed, and whom the Father hath sent to all those who believe in and love His Son.

All the preliminary steps in grace, all the elementary blessings in Christian experience, are the preparation of the soul for the reception of the Holy Ghost. It is fitting up and preparing the temple for His dwelling place. The reception of God in the third person of the Trinity into the soul is a climax in the history of personal redemption. It is a sealing of the heart for eternal glory. It is the reception of the Sanctifier, Comforter, Revealer, Teacher and Guide, sent by the Father in answer to the prayer of His Son to cleanse, sanctify, and keep His followers from the evil one, and by His incoming and abiding to prepare them for residence in the New Jerusalem.

The willful and final rejection of the Holy Ghost would prove destructive and fatal to all Christian experience.

"I will therefore put you in remembrance, though ye once knew this, how that the Lord having saved the people out of the land of Egypt, afterward destroyed them that believed not."—*Jude*.

The grace that one receives at justification does not justify that one in the rejection of the additional grace to be bestowed in the development and perfection of experience, and Christian character, but it obligates the soul thus justified to go forward searching out, seeking after, and submitting to all the will of God.

"Now the just shall live by faith, but if any

man draw back, my soul shall have no pleasure in him." Heb. 10:38.

Reader, there comes a time in the history of every justified believer, when the Father will answer the prayer of the Son, and send to that believer the Comforter. The Holy Ghost is the promise of the Father, and the promise of the Father shall not fail. He will come suddenly into His temple. Woe will be to the soul that rejects Him when He comes.

God is longsuffering. Patiently He will wait, earnestly will He entreat; the Spirit will knock again and again for admittance and full control of the believer's heart, but God has said: "My Spirit shall not always strive with man." Repeatedly rejected, He will finally take His departure to return no more. Then the poor soul will find its house desolate indeed. Having rejected Comforter, Guide, Cleanser, Empowerer and Teacher, its condition is sad to contemplate.

The last person in the Trinity has come, been trifled with, rejected, grieved, and has finally taken His departure from those who would not receive Him in His sanctifying and indwelling power.

The last state of such a soul is worse than the first. May God in mercy help the reader of these pages now to make so complete a consecration, and to exercise so strong a faith, that the Holy Ghost, in His sanctifying and keeping power may enter into his or her heart in all His blessed fullness, and never hence depart.

EXPERIENCES

That the reader may understand that the views set forth in the preceding chapters are not peculiar to the author of this booklet, I will give in this chapter several quotations from distinguished Christian scholars, whose views and teachings are quite in harmony with the main thought of what I have written.

First, I will quote a paragraph from a work on "The Holy Spirit," by the Rev. John Owen, D. D., some time vice-chancellor of the University of Oxford, an eminent Presbyterian minister. On pages 222 and 223 of this work, under the head of "The Positive Work of the Spirit in the Sanctification of Believers," we find the following:

"We now proceed to the positive work of the Spirit in the sanctification of believers; for he not only cleanses their natures and persons from the pollution of sin, but he communicates the great, permanent, positive effect of holiness to their souls, whereby he guides and assists them in all the acts and duties thereof.

"I shall comprise what belongs to this part of his work in the two following propositions:

"1. There is in the soul of believers a supernatural principle or habit of grace, wrought and preserved by the Spirit of God, whereby they are enabled to live unto God, and perform that obedience which He requires and accepts, and this is essentially distinct from all natural habits, intellectual or moral, however acquired or improved.

"2. There is an immediate work of the Holy

Spirit required unto every act of holy obedience, whether external or internal.   (p. 226). We may learn from hence how great and excellent a work this of sanctification is, and that it is a greater matter to be truly holy than most persons are aware of. It is so great a work that it must be wrought by 'the God of peace Himself,' by the blood of Christ, and by the influence of the Spirit."

The pious reader will be pleased with the following from the pen of that eminent Methodist preacher, Rev. William Arthur, A.M. We read on pages 62, 63 and 64, of "The Tongue of Fire" (a book that all Christians should read):

"What a labor of expression do we find in 2 Cor. 9:8, where Paul wants to convey his own idea of the power of grace, as practically enabling men to do the will of God. 'And God is able to make all grace abound toward you; that ye, always having all sufficiency in all things may abound to every good work.' Here we have 'abound' twice, and 'all' four times in one short sentence. 'Abound' means not only to fill, but to overthrow. The double overflow, first of grace from God to us, then of the same grace from us to 'every good work' is a glorious comment on our Lord's word: 'He that believeth on me, as the Scriptures hath said, out of his belly shall flow rivers of living water. But this spake He of the Spirit, which they that believed on Him should receive; for the Holy Ghost was not yet given, because that Jesus was not yet glorified.' The believer's heart, in itself, incapable of holy living,

as a marble cistern of yielding a constant stream,
is placed like a cistern in communication with an
invisible source; the source constantly overflows
into the cistern, and it again overflows. Happy the
heart thus filled, thus overflowing with the Holy
Spirit! Where is the fountain of those living wa-
ters that we may bring our hearts thither? 'He
showed me a pure river of water of life clear as
crystal, proceeding out of the throne of God and
of the Lamb.' (Rev. 22:1). There is the fountain, there the stream: the Spirit proceeding from
the Father and the Son to the throne of grace! to
the mercy seat! and you are at the fountain of all
life. Nor seek a scant supply at that source. 'Be
filled with the Spirit,' sounds in your ears, and if
you believe, not only will a well 'spring up within' you, but rivers shall flow out from you. The
Spirit, as replenishing the believer's heart with
actual virtues and practical holiness, is ever kept
before our eye in the apostolic writings. 'That ye
may walk worthy of the Lord unto all pleasing,
being fruitful in every good work, and increasing
in the knowledge of God: strengthened with all
might, according to His glorious power, unto all
patience and longsuffering with joyfulness.' Put-
ting these various expressions together, what a
view do they give of the riches of grace! 'all sufficiency' 'in all things,' 'always,' 'abound to every
good work,' 'fruitful in every good work,'
'strengthened with all might,' 'according to
His glorious power, 'according to the power that
worketh in us,' 'filled with all the fulness of
God,' Eternal Spirit proceeding from the Father

and the Son, answer and disperse all our unbelief by filling our hearts with Thyself. The expression 'filled with the Holy Ghost,' places before us the human spirit restored to its original and highest fellowship."

In speaking of how to obtain this experience, Mr. Arthur says, on pages 320 and 321:

"As to the way in which this power may be obtained here we have only to recall the lesson of the ten days—'they continued with one accord in prayer and supplication.' Prayer earnest, prayer united, and prayer persevering—these are the conditions, and these fulfilled, we shall assuredly be 'endued with power from on high.'"

Nothing could be more plainly set forth than Mr. Arthur's teaching here that the Holy Ghost is to be sought and obtained in answer to prayer, by believing Christians.

Perhaps no pastor in the United States, in the last quarter of a century, was more widely known, and more genuinely beloved, than the Rev. A. J. Gordon, a Baptist minister of Boston, who walked with God, and was not, for God took him up to Himself. In an excellent little volume entitled, "The Ministry of the Spirit," on page 76, Mr. Gordon says:

"It seems clear from the Scriptures that it is still the duty and privilege of believers to receive the Holy Spirit by a conscious, definite act of appropriating faith, just as they received Jesus."

On page 92 he says:

"It seems to me beyond question, as a matter of experience, both of Christians in the present day and of the early Church, as recorded by inspiration, that in addition to the gift of the Spirit received at conversion, there is another blessing corresponding in its signs and effects to the blessing received by the disciples at Pentecost—a blessing to be asked for and expected by Christians still, and to be described in language similar to that employed in the book of the Acts. Whatever that blessing may be, it is in immediate connection with the Holy Ghost."

On page 98 he says:

"It is easy to cite cases of decisive, vivid, and clearly marked experience of the Spirit's endorsement, as in the lives of Dr. Finney, James Brainard Taylor, and many others. And instead of describing these experiences—so definite as to time and so distinct as to accompanying credentials—we would ask the reader to study them, and observe the remarkable effects which followed in the ministry of those who enjoyed them. The lives of many of the co-laborers with Wesley and Whitefield give a striking confirmation of the doctrine which we are defending."

The late Phillips Brooks, Bishop in the Protestant Episcopal Church, reaches a beautiful climax in a sermon on Acts 19:2, in these impressive words:

"But here at Pentecost, what was there to call out such prodigies? If what we have said is true, was there not certainly enough? It was the coming back of God into man. It was the promise in these typical men of how near God would be to every man henceforth. It was the manifestation

of the God Inspirer as distinct from and yet one
with God Creator, and God Redeemer. It was
primarily the entrance of God into man, and so,
in consequence, the entrance of its spirit and full
meaning into every truth man could know. It was
the blossom-day of humanity, full of the promise
of unmeasured fruit. And what that first Whit-
Sunday was to all the world, one certain day
comes to any man the day that the Holy Spirit
comes to him. God enters into him, and he sees
everything with God's vision."

On December 26, 1899, funeral services were
held over the remains of Dwight L. Moody, at
Northfield, Mass. One of the principal spokesmen
on that occasion was Dr. Schofield. Among other
things he said:

"The secret of Dwight L. Moody's power lay:

"First—In a definite experience of Christ's
saving grace. He had passed out of death into
life and he knew it.

"Secondly—Mr. Moody believed in the Divine
authority of the Scriptures. The Bible was to
him the voice of God, and he made it resound as
such in the consciences of men.

"Thirdly—*He was baptized with the Holy
Spirit, and he knew that he was. It was to him
as definite an experience as his conversion.*

"Fourthly—He was a man of prayer. He believed in a living and unfettered God.

"But, Fifthly—Mr. Moody believed in work, in
ceaseless effort, in wise provision, in the power of
organization, of publicity. I like to think of
Dwight L. Moody in heaven. I like to think of

him with his Lord, and with Elijah, Daniel, Paul, Augustine, Luther, Wesley and Finney.

"Farewell, for a little time, great heart, may a double portion of the Spirit be vouchsafed to us who remain."

I call the attention of the reader especially to the fact that Dr. Schofield said, *"He was baptized with the Holy Spirit, and knew that he was. It was to him as definite an experience as his conversion."*

Mr. Moody himself says:

"The blessing came upon me suddenly like a flash of lightning. For months I had been hungering and thirsting for power in service. I had come to that point that I think I would have died if I had not got it. I remember I was walking the streets of New York. I had no more heart in the business I was about than if I had not belonged to the world at all. Right there, on the street, the power of God seemed to come upon me so wonderfully that I had to ask God to stay His hand. I was filled with a sense of God's goodness, and I felt as though I could take the whole world to my heart. I took the old sermons I had preached before without any power; it was the same old truth, but there was new power. Many were impressed and converted. This happened years after I was converted myself."

These quotations will suffice. The doctrine of the baptism with the Holy Ghost is not only a Bible doctrine, but is taught and experienced by the most devout men of all the evangelical churches.

www.ingramcontent.com/pod-product-compliance
Lightning Source LLC
Chambersburg PA
CBHW030308030426
42337CB00012B/634